THIS BOOK BELONGS TO

Once upon a time,
in a cozy meadow surrounded by tall,
whispering trees,
lived a little bunny named Ella.

Ella was a soft, fluffy bunny with big,
bright eyes and a twitchy little nose.

She loved hopping around the meadow,
exploring all the wonderful things nature
had to offer.

One day, as the sun was setting and the sky turned a beautiful shade of pink, bunny Ella decided to go on a little adventure.

She hopped out of her warm, leafy bed and into the cool evening air.

The stars were just starting to twinkle, and the moon was beginning to rise, casting a gentle glow over the meadow

Ella hopped along a soft, winding path, her ears twitching with excitement.

She saw her favorite flowers, the ones that smelled like honey, and she stopped to sniff them.

Then, she spotted a family of friendly
fireflies dancing in the air.

Ella watched in wonder
as they flickered and flew,
lighting up the night like tiny stars.

As Bella continued her adventure, she heard a soft rustling sound.

She followed the sound and soon found a little mouse named Max, who was gathering seeds for his dinner.

"Hello, Ella," said Max. "Are you out on an adventure?"

"Yes," said Ella, smiling.

"I'm exploring the meadow at night.

It's so magical!"

Max nodded. "It is indeed. But be careful not to wander too far. Night-time can be a little tricky."

Ella thanked Max and continued on her way.

She hopped and hopped until she reached the edge of the meadow, where the trees stood tall and silent.

Ella peered into the woods, feeling a little nervous.

The trees looked so big and mysterious in the dark.

But then she remembered what Max had said and decided not to go any further.

Just as she was about to turn back,
Ella heard a soft, gentle hoot.

It was Owl, who lived in one of the tall
trees.

"Hello, Ella,"

Owl said kindly.

"What brings you to the edge of the
woods?"

"I was just exploring," Ella replied.

"But I think it's time for me to go home."

Owl nodded wisely.
"That's a good idea.

The night is beautiful, but it's important to be safe.

Why don't I fly above you and light your way back home with my soft feathers?"

Ella felt relieved and happy. "Thank you, Owl," she said.

With Owl flying above, Ella hopped back along the path, feeling safe and sound.

The moonlight guided her, and the stars twinkled brighter than ever.

Ella thought about all the wonderful things she had seen on her adventure: the sweet-smelling flowers, the dancing fireflies, and her new friend Max.

Soon, Ella was back in her cozy bed, snuggled up in the soft leaves.

Owl landed on a branch nearby and whispered, "Goodnight, little bunny. Sweet dreams."

"Goodnight, Owl," Ella whispered back.

And as Ella drifted off to sleep

she dreamed of more adventures in the meadow,

knowing that no matter where she

went, she was always safe and loved.

zzZ

THE

END